Alaska

Government & Boroughs websites

Paul F. Davis

Alaska has a longer coastline than all the other United States combined. At 663,268 square miles (1,717,856 km²) in total area, Alaska is by far the largest state in the United States. Alaska is more than twice the size of the second-largest U.S. state (Texas) and is larger than the next three largest states (Texas, California, and Montana) combined. Alaska is the seventh largest subnational division in the world. If Alaska was an independent nation, it would be the 18th largest country in the world, almost the same size as Iran.

With its myriad islands, Alaska has nearly 34,000 miles (55,000 km) of tidal shoreline. The Aleutian Islands chain extends west from the southern tip of the Alaska Peninsula. Many active volcanoes are found in the Aleutians and in coastal regions. Unimak Island is home to Mount Shishaldin, an occasionally smoldering volcano that rises to 10,000 feet (3,000 m) above the North Pacific.

The state of Alaska has 29 boroughs accounting for and governmentally managing the great state. Alaska has more than three million lakes. The Bering Glacier is the largest glacier in North America, covering 2,008 square miles (5,200 km^2) alone.

Alaska has a total of 355 incorporated cities and census-designated places (CDPs).

Alaska has the lowest individual tax burden in the United States. Alaska is one of the five states with no sales tax and one of seven states with no individual income tax. To finance state government operations, Alaska depends primarily on petroleum revenues and federal subsidies. The Tax Foundation has ranked Alaska as the fourth most business friendly state in the nation based on its tax policy.

Alaska has the 5th largest number of millionaires per capita in the United States. The oil and gas industry dominates the Alaskan economy, with more than 80% of the state's revenues derived from petroleum extraction. Alaska's main exports (excluding oil and natural gas) are seafood, salmon, cod, pollock and crab.

Alaska has over 21,000 employer establishments, which employ over 316,000 people, contributing to generating $55 billion annually for the state. Agricultural production is primarily for consumption within the state and includes nursery stock, dairy products, vegetables, and livestock. Manufacturing is limited, with most foodstuffs and general goods imported from elsewhere.

Employment is primarily in government and industries such as natural resource extraction, shipping, and transportation. Military bases are a significant component of the economy in the Fairbanks North Star, Anchorage and Kodiak Island boroughs, as well as Kodiak.

Federal subsidies are also an important part of the economy, allowing the state to keep taxes low. Its industrial outputs are crude petroleum, natural gas, coal, gold, precioius metals, zinc, seafood, timber and wood products. Alaska's tourism sector is also growing, while being supported by local lodging.

Among Alaska's popular annual events are the *Iditarod Trail Sled Dog Race* from Anchorage to Nome, *World Ice Art Championships* in Fairbanks, the *Blueberry*

Festival and *Alaska Hummingbird Festival* in Ketchian, the *Sitka Whale Fest*, and the *Stikine River Garnet Fest* in Wrangell. The Stikine River attracts the largest spring concentration of American bald eagles in the world.

The *Alaska Native Arts Foundation* markets and promotes Native, while the *Alaska Native Heritage Center* celebrates the rich heritage of Alaska's 11 cultural groups. Cross-cultural exchange among all people is encouraged to enhance the self-esteem among Native people.

The tally of cities includes four unified municipalities, the majority of these communities being located in the rural expanse of Alaska known as "the bush" and are unconnected to that contiguous North American road network.

One of the world's largest tides occurs in Turnagain Arm, just south of Anchorage, where tidal differences can be more than 35 feet (10.7 m). Not part of the contiguous United States, often referred to as "the lower 48," Alaska is not connected by road to the rest of the North American highway system.

Approximately half of Alaska's residents live within the Anchorage metropolitan area. Indigenous people have lived in Alaska for thousands of years, and it is widely believed that the region served as the entry point for the initial settlement of North America by way of the Bering land bridge.

The Russian Empire was the first to actively colonize the area of Alaska beginning in the 18th century, eventually establishing Russian America, which spanned most of the current state, and promoted and maintained a native Alaskan Creole population.

The expense and logistical difficulty of maintaining this distant possession prompted Russia to sale Alaska to the United States in 1867 for $7.2 million (equivalent to $140 million in 2021). The area went through several administrative changes before becoming organized as a territory on May 11, 1912. Alaska was admitted as the 49th state of the U.S. on January 3, 1959.

Abundant natural resources have enabled Alaska—with one of the smallest state economies—to have one of the highest per capita incomes, with commercial fishing, the extraction of natural gas and oil, dominating the Alaska economy.

U.S. Armed Forces bases and tourism also contribute to the economy. More than half of Alaska has federally owned land containing wildlife refuges, national parks and national forests.

The Alaska National Interest Lands Conservation Act (ANILCA) of 1980 added 53.7 million acres (217,000 km^2) to the National Wildlife Refuge system, parts of 25 rivers to the National Wild and Scenic Rivers system, 3.3 million acres (13,000 km^2) to National Forest lands, and 43.6 million acres (176,000 km^2) to National Park land. Because of the Act, Alaska now contains two-thirds of all American national parklands. Today, more than half of Alaskan land is owned by the Federal Government. The United States Bureau of Land Management has reported that approximately 65% of Alaska is owned and managed by the U.S. federal government.

Of the remaining land area, the state of Alaska owns 101 million acres (41 million hectares), its entitlement under the Alaska Statehood Act. The University of Alaska, a land grant university, also owns substantial acreage which it manages independently.

Alaska has vast energy resources, although some have been depleted over the years. Major oil and gas reserves were found in the Alaska North Slope (ANS) and Cook Inlet basins.

The Trans-Alaska Pipeline can transport and pump up to 2.1 million barrels (330,000 m³) of crude oil per day, more than any other crude oil pipeline in the United

States. Additionally, substantial coal deposits are found in Alaska's bituminous, sub-bituminous, and lignite coal basins. The U.S. Geological Survey estimates that there are 85.4 trillion cubic feet (2,420 km^3) of undiscovered, technically recoverable gas from natural gas hydrates on the Alaskan North Slope.

Alaska also offers some of the highest hydroelectric power potential in the nation from its several rivers. Large swaths of the Alaskan coastline offer wind and geothermal energy potential as well.

The cost of goods in Alaska has long been higher than in the contiguous 48 states.

Federal government employees, particularly the United States Postal (USPS) workers and active-duty military members, receive a Cost of Living Allowance usually set at 25% of base pay because, while the cost of living has gone down, it is still one of the highest in the country. Rural Alaska suffers from extremely high prices for food and consumer goods compared to the rest of the country, due to the relatively limited transportation infrastructure.

Alaska has an abundance of seafood, with the primary fisheries in the Bering Sea and the North Pacific. Seafood is one of the few food items that is often cheaper within the state than outside it. Many Alaskans take advantage of salmon seasons to harvest portions of their household diet while fishing for subsistence, as well as sport.

Hunting for subsistence, primarily caribou, moose, and Dall sheep is common in the Alaskan bush communities. A traditional native food is Akutaq, Eskimo ice cream, which can consist of reindeer fat, seal oil, dried fish meat and local berries.

Source:

https://en.wikipedia.org/wiki/Alaska

Paul F. Davis is an international educator, worldwide minister, inspirational speaker and author of 100 books. Paul has traveled throughout the United States and to 90 nations of the world.

Paul's father was a real estate appraiser, broker, and home builder. Thus, Paul grew up with a keen understanding of real estate law, state and county jurisdiction, building codes and the nuances of pulling a permit when constructing and remodeling homes with his father. Paul also earned a Master degree in Law from Michigan State College of Law, where he earned a jurisprudence award within the field of Administrative Law, related to federal government agencies, policy and protocol.

For this reason, Paul as a world traveler took interest in researching the state of Alaska to ascertain the many government and counties' websites to assist politicians, entrepreneurs, business and community leaders, real estate developers, urban planners, families, citizens and others seeking to relocate to the area to easily find the government offices and officials in authority who can best serve their needs and the respective agencies therein who can advance their interests.

This timeless and priceless resource will be an asset to governments, multinational companies, CEOs, executives, business and community leaders, entrepreneurs, real estate developers, urban planners, aspiring and seasoned politicians, nonprofit organizations, churches, social service workers and grant writers eager to network with brokers of power and partner with those with positions of influence capable of bringing about positive change within their respective areas of interest.

Sometimes with elections come power shifts and changes in government. Thankfully, most government websites remain the same and do not change despite changes in governmental leadership. Nevertheless, sometimes due to cyber security issues, distrust and insecurities in leadership; politicians may propose, opt, or pursue website url changes to feel more at ease regarding possible data breaches, prevent hacking and give them more peace of mind amid political opposition (who perhaps previously ran the website, mined and managed the online data). For this reason, I respectfully apologize if in the future a website previously in operation suddenly ceases to work, as such is beyond my control. Nevertheless, if and when a county website was tough to locate, I often added a couple of websites (sometimes several) to track different aspects of county government operations and their respective offices to at minimum lead you in the right direction (and often therewith provide some valuable bonus sites with unique data that will further enlighten you as to the region, the economic opportunities therein, future development, desirable places to visit, interesting sites to explore, and the area's overall potential). The county websites are listed last at the end of this document, should you wish to find them first.

"A wise man will hear, and will
increase learning; and a man of understanding
shall attain unto wise counsels" (Proverbs 1:5).

"Give instruction to a wise man, and he will be
yet wiser: teach a just man, and he will
increase in learning" (Proverbs 9:9).

"The wise in heart shall be called prudent:
and the sweetness of the lips
increase learning" (Proverbs 16:21).

"The heart of the wise teaches his mouth, and adds learning to his lips" (Proverbs 16:23).

"Give attendance to reading, to exhortation, to doctrine" (1Timothy 4:13).

Paul F. Davis is a global business consultant, worldwide inspirational speaker, international educator (licensed in Florida and California) and UCLA certified University and Career Counselor. Paul speaks for governments, companies and universities worldwide on a number of topics.

PaulFDavis.com
EducationPro.us
Tinyurl.com/PaulFDavis-Books
DreamMakerMinistries.com
PropheticPowerShift.com
RevivingNations@yahoo,com

Please email Paul to check his availability to speak in your city and/or provide consulting services.

Hereafter are over 18 pages
of websites for the state of Alaska
government and its respective counties
to easily access.

Official Alaska State Website
https://alaska.gov/

Alaska State Government
https://www.usa.gov/state-government/alaska

U.S. Department of State in Alaska
https://www.state.gov/states/alaska/

https://2017-2021.state.gov/states/alaska/index.html

U.S. Attorney's Office – District of Alaska
https://www.justice.gov/usao-ak

Governor of Alaska

https://gov.alaska.gov/

https://www.nga.org/governor/mike-dunleavy/

https://www.facebook.com/GovDunleavy/

https://twitter.com/govdunleavy?lang=en

https://www.instagram.com/govdunleavy/

https://www.pbs.org/newshour/politics/mike-dunleavy-becomes-1st-alaska-governor-reelected-since-1998

Alaska – Office of the Lieutenant Governor

https://akleg.gov/docs/pdf/doso/dosoALL.pdf#page=38

State of Alaska – Online Public Notices

https://aws.state.ak.us/OnlinePublicNotices/

Alaska Attorney General

https://www.naag.org/attorney-general/treg-taylor/#:~:text=Alaska%20Attorney%20General&text=Attorney%20General%20Treg%20Taylor%20started,charge%20of%20the%20civil%20division

https://www.stateagreport.com/states/alaska/

https://environmentamerica.org/alaska/updates/alaskas-attorney-general-joins-call-for-right-to-repair-legislation/

Alaska State Legislature – Directory of Officials
https://akleg.gov/pubs/doso.php

Alaska Legislative Affairs Agency
https://akleg.gov/docs/pdf/doso/dosoALL.pdf#page=24

Alaska Legislative Agencies
https://akleg.gov/docs/pdf/doso/dosoALL.pdf#page=30

Alaska Congressional Delegation
https://akleg.gov/docs/pdf/doso/dosoALL.pdf#page=10

Alaska Department of Administration

https://doa.alaska.gov/

https://www.facebook.com/alaska.doa/

https://akleg.gov/docs/pdf/doso/dosoALL.pdf#page=40

Alaska Department of Commerce, Community and Economic Development

https://www.commerce.alaska.gov/web/

https://akleg.gov/docs/pdf/doso/dosoALL.pdf#page=50

Alaska Department of Natural Resources

https://akleg.gov/docs/pdf/doso/dosoALL.pdf#page=136

Alaska Department of Environmental Conservation

https://dec.alaska.gov/

https://akleg.gov/docs/pdf/doso/dosoALL.pd
f#page=74

U.S. EPA – Climate Impacts on Alaska
https://19january2017snapshot.epa.gov/clima
te-impacts/climate-impacts-alaska_.html

USDA – Alaska and a Changing Climate
https://www.climatehubs.usda.gov/hubs/nort
hwest/topic/alaska-and-changing-climate
Alaska – Global Change
https://nca2014.globalchange.gov/report/regi
ons/alaska

**Environment and Natural Resources
Institute**
https://www.uaa.alaska.edu/academics/colle
ge-of-arts-and-
sciences/programs/environment-and-natural-
resources-institute/index.cshtml

Alaska Department of Fish and Game
https://www.adfg.alaska.gov/

https://secure.wildlife.alaska.gov/index.cfm?
adfg=harvest.main

https://akleg.gov/docs/pdf/doso/dosoALL.pdf#page=78

Alaska Department of Family and Community Services

https://akleg.gov/docs/pdf/doso/dosoALL.pdf#page=78

Alaska Department of Education and Early Development

https://akleg.gov/docs/pdf/doso/dosoALL.pdf#page=68

Alaska Department of Health and Social Services

https://dhss.alaska.gov/Pages/default.aspx

https://health.alaska.gov/

https://www.fns.usda.gov/fns-contact/alaska-department-health-social-services-administration

https://peerta.acf.hhs.gov/content/alaska-department-health-social-services

https://npin.cdc.gov/organization/alaska-department-health-and-social-services-1

https://www.linkedin.com/company/alaskadhss/

https://www.facebook.com/doh.alaska/

https://www.youtube.com/channel/UCdSFkhEfw_r1Tmbze25bq2A

Alaska Department of Health Services
https://health.alaska.gov/Pages/Services.aspx

Alaska Medicare & Medicaid Services
https://www.cms.gov/contacts/alaska-department-health-and-social-services/general-professional-contact/1563011

Anchorage Health Department
https://www.muni.org/departments/health/Pages/default.aspx

Alaska Department of Law
https://law.alaska.gov/

https://akleg.gov/docs/pdf/doso/dosoALL.pdf#page=122

Alaska Department of Military & Veterans Affairs

https://akleg.gov/docs/pdf/doso/dosoALL.pdf#page=128

Alaska Department of Public Safety

https://akleg.gov/docs/pdf/doso/dosoALL.pdf#page=140

Department of Transportation & Public Facilities

https://akleg.gov/docs/pdf/doso/dosoALL.pdf#page=154

Alaska Department of Revenue

https://akleg.gov/docs/pdf/doso/dosoALL.pdf#page=146

Alaska Court System

https://akleg.gov/docs/pdf/doso/dosoALL.pdf#page=162

Alaska Department of Corrections

https://akleg.gov/docs/pdf/doso/dosoALL.pdf#page=60

Alaska Boroughs and Census Areas

https://live.laborstats.alaska.gov/pop/estimates/pub/chap2.pdf

Aleutians East Borough - Alaska

https://www.aleutianseast.org/

Aleutians West Census Area - Alaska

https://www.census.gov/quickfacts/fact/table/aleutianswestcensusareaalaska/AGE295221
https://www.ahfc.us/application/files/5115/1510/4546/Final_-_Aleutians_West_Census_Area_Summary.pdf

https://swamc.org/about/regional-profile/aleutians-west-census-area/
https://www.aleutianswest.org/

Anchorage Municipality - Alaska

https://www.muni.org/

Bethel - Alaska

https://www.cityofbethel.org/

https://www.census.gov/quickfacts/bethelcensusareaalaska

https://explorenorth.com/library/communities/alaska/bl-Bethel.htm

Bristol Bay Borough - Alaska

http://www.bristolbayboroughak.us/

Denali Borough - Alaska

https://denaliborough.govoffice.com/

Dillingham - Alaska

https://www.dillinghamak.us/

Fairbanks North Star Borough - Alaska

https://www.fnsb.gov/

Haines Borough - Alaska

https://www.hainesalaska.gov/

Hoonah-Angoon - Alaska

https://www.cityofhoonah.org/

https://dot.alaska.gov/amhs/comm/sevillage
s.shtml

https://cityofangoon.org/

https://www.hoonah-angoon.org/

Juneau City and Borough - Alaska

https://beta.juneau.org/

Kenai Peninsula Borough - Alaska

https://www.kpb.us/

Ketchikan Gateway Borough - Alaska

https://www.kgbak.us/

Kodiak Island Borough - Alaska

https://www.kodiakak.us/

Lake and Peninsula Borough - Alaska

https://www.lakeandpen.com/

https://education.alaska.gov/information-exchange-blog/better-together-lake-and-peninsula-borough-school-district

https://education.alaska.gov/DOE_Rolodex/SchoolCalendar/District/30

Matanuska-Susitna Borough - Alaska

https://www.matsugov.us/

Nome - Alaska

https://www.nomealaska.org/

North Slope Borough - Alaska

https://www.north-slope.org/

https://www.north-slope.org/departments/

Northwest Arctic Borough - Alaska

https://www.nwabor.org/

Petersburg Borough - Alaska

https://www.petersburgak.gov/

Prince of Wales-Hyder - Alaska

https://courts.alaska.gov/courtdir/1pw.htm

http://live.laborstats.alaska.gov/cen/maps/bor/current/198.pdf

https://www.powhsd.org/

Sitka City and Borough - Alaska

https://www.cityofsitka.com/

Municipality of Skagway Borough - Alaska

https://www.skagway.org/

Southeast Fairbanks - Alaska

https://www.census.gov/quickfacts/fact/table/southeastfairbankscensusareaalaska/PST045221

https://datausa.io/profile/geo/southeast-fairbanks-census-area-ak

https://www.inaturalist.org/places/southeast-fairbanks-county

https://www.sefairbanks.us/

Unorganized Borough - Alaska

https://www.commerce.alaska.gov/web/portals/4/pub/Model_Boro_RPT.pdf

https://www.congress.gov/congressional-report/104th-congress/senate-report/396/1

https://commons.wikimedia.org/wiki/File:Map_of_Alaska_highlighting_the_Unorganized_Borough.svg

https://law.justia.com/codes/alaska/2018/title-29/chapter-03/

https://www.cntraveler.com/stories/2016-02-01/13-percent-of-alaskans-live-in-no-mans-land

https://www.akml.org/wp-content/uploads/2020/11/Unorganized-Borough-Walker.pdf
https://www.commerce.alaska.gov/web/dcra/UnorganizedBorough.aspx

Valdez-Cordova - Alaska

https://www.valdezak.gov/

https://datausa.io/profile/geo/valdez-cordova-census-area-ak

https://www.niche.com/places-to-live/c/valdez-cordova-borough-ak/

https://www.cvalaska.com/

Wrangell City and Borough - Alaska

https://www.wrangell.com/

Yakutat City and Borough - Alaska

https://yakutatak.govoffice2.com/

https://www.facebook.com/Admin99689/

https://www.census.gov/quickfacts/fact/table
/yakutatcityandboroughalaska,US/HSG49522
1

https://www.akml.org/wp-
content/uploads/2021/02/City-Borough-of-
Yakutat.pdf

https://www.yakutatak.gov/

Yukon-Koyukuk - Alaska

https://www.census.gov/quickfacts/fact/table/yukonkoyukukcensusareaalaska,matanuskasusitnaboroughalaska,AK/BZA010220

https://education.alaska.gov/DOE_Rolodex/SchoolCalendar/District/52
https://fred.stlouisfed.org/series/GDPGOVT02290

https://pubs.usgs.gov/bul/0631/report.pdf

https://www.census.gov/quickfacts/fact/table/yukonkoyukukcensusareaalaska/PST045222

https://www.commerce.alaska.gov/web/dcra/
News.aspx

https://labor.alaska.gov/trends/trendspdf/fe
b01.pdf
https://www.formalu.com/us/alaska/yukon-
koyukuk

https://www.yksd.com/

https://lawyers.law.cornell.edu/lawyers/gove
rnment-administrative-law/alaska/yukon-
koyukuk-county

Thank you for reading this book. If you know of any other Alaska government websites you would like to add to this book, you are welcome to email Paul and suggest they be added.

If you would like to hire Paul to research a particular aspect of the state of Alaska, a specific county, economy, industry, provide a report and/or evaluation on the viability of a business proposal or venture; please email Paul to discuss the matter further.

Paul F. Davis is a global business consultant, worldwide minister, inspirational speaker, international educator (licensed in Florida and California) and UCLA certified University and Career Counselor. Paul speaks for governments, companies and universities worldwide on a number of topics.

PaulFDavis.com
EducationPro.us
Tinyurl.com/PaulFDavis-Books
RevivingNations@yahoo/com

Please email Paul to check his availability to speak in your city and/or provide consulting services.